Going Around the Big Apple

You're
NEW YORK

Experience Travel Journal

Activinotes

Activinotes

DAILY JOURNALS, PLANNERS, NOTEBOOKS AND OTHER BLANK BOOKS

Travel Journal

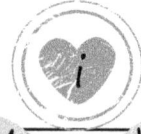

New York

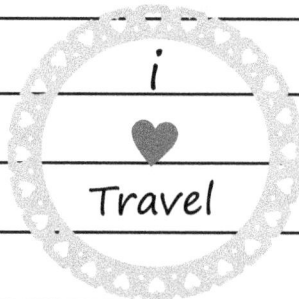
i ♥ Travel

Travel Journal

New York

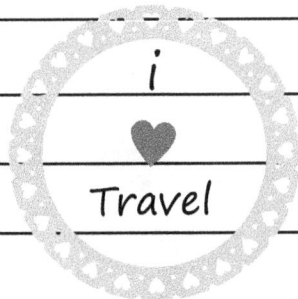

i

♥

Travel

Travel Journal

i ♥ New York

Things to See & Do:

☐ ....
☐ ....
☐ ....
☐ ....
☐ ....
☐ ....
☐ ....
☐ ....
☐ ....
☐ ....

Things to Observe :

....
....
....
....
....
....
....

Adventures to Have :

....
....
....
....
....
....
....

i ♥ Travel

Places to Mingle :

....
....
....
....
....
....
....

Travel Journal

Shops to Visit :

....
....
....
....
....
....
....

Streets to Check out :

....
....
....
....
....
....
....

People to Meet :

....
....
....
....
....
....
....

Travel Journal

New York

i

♥

Travel

Travel Journal

DATE: /   /

Things to See & Do.

- ☐ ....
- ☐ ....
- ☐ ....
- ☐ ....
- ☐ ....
- ☐ ....
- ☐ ....
- ☐ ....
- ☐ ....
- ☐ ....

i ♥ New York

Things to Observe :

....
....
....
....
....
....
....

Adventures to Have :

....
....
....
....
....
....
....

i ♥ Travel

Places to Mingle :

....
....
....
....
....
....
....

Travel Journal

Shops to Visit :

....
....
....
....
....
....
....

Streets to Check out :

....
....
....
....
....
....
....

People to Meet :

....
....
....
....
....
....
....

Travel Journal

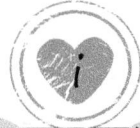 

New York

_____
_____
_____
_____
_____
_____
_____
_____
_____
_____
_____
_____
_____
_____
_____
_____
_____
_____
_____
_____

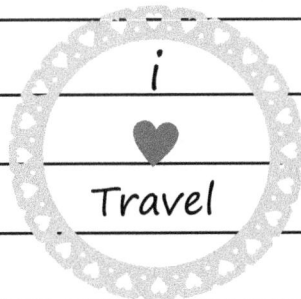

i ♥ Travel

Travel Journal

Things to See & Do:

- ☐ ....
- ☐ ....
- ☐ ....
- ☐ ....
- ☐ ....
- ☐ ....
- ☐ ....
- ☐ ....
- ☐ ....
- ☐ ....

i ♥ New York

Things to Observe :

....
....
....
....
....
....
....

Adventures to Have :

....
....
....
....
....
....

i ♥ Travel

Places to Mingle :

....
....
....
....
....
....
....

Travel Journal

New York

Shops to Visit :

....
....
....
....
....
....
....

Streets to Check out :

....
....
....
....
....
....
....

People to Meet :

....
....
....
....
....
....
....

Travel Journal

New York

i ♥ Travel

Travel Journal

i ♥ New York

Things to See & Do:

☐ ....
☐ ....
☐ ....
☐ ....
☐ ....
☐ ....
☐ ....
☐ ....
☐ ....
☐ ....

Things to Observe :

....
....
....
....
....
....
....

Adventures to Have :

....
....
....
....
....
....

i ♥ Travel

Places to Mingle :

....
....
....
....
....
....
....

Travel Journal

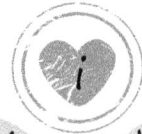

New York

Shops to Visit :

....
....
....
....
....
....
....

Streets to Check out :

....
....
....
....
....
....
....

People to Meet :

....
....
....
....
....
....
....

Travel Journal

New York

i ♥ Travel

Travel Journal

DATE: /   /

i ♥ New York

Things to See & Do:

- ☐ ....
- ☐ ....
- ☐ ....
- ☐ ....
- ☐ ....
- ☐ ....
- ☐ ....
- ☐ ....
- ☐ ....
- ☐ ....

Things to Observe :

....
....
....
....
....
....
....

Adventures to Have :

....
....
....
....
....
....
....

i ♥ Travel

Places to Mingle :

....
....
....
....
....
....
....

Travel Journal

Shops to Visit :

....
....
....
....
....
....
....

Streets to Check out :

....
....
....
....
....
....
....

People to Meet :

....
....
....
....
....
....
....

Travel Journal

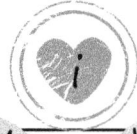 

 New York

i ♥ Travel

Travel Journal

I ❤ New York

Things to See & Do:

- [ ] ....
- [ ] ....
- [ ] ....
- [ ] ....
- [ ] ....
- [ ] ....
- [ ] ....
- [ ] ....
- [ ] ....
- [ ] ....

Things to Observe :

....
....
....
....
....
....
....

Adventures to Have :

....
....
....
....
....
....
....

i ❤ Travel

Places to Mingle :

....
....
....
....
....
....
....

Travel Journal

Shops to Visit :

....
....
....
....
....
....

Streets to Check out :

....
....
....
....
....
....
....

People to Meet :

....
....
....
....
....
....
....

Travel Journal

New York

_____
_____
_____
_____
_____
_____
_____
_____
_____
_____
_____
_____
_____
_____
_____
_____
_____
_____

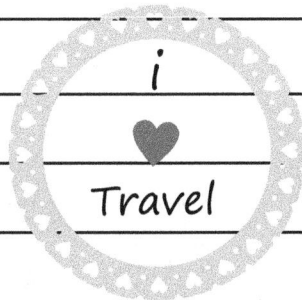

i

♥

Travel

Travel Journal

Things to See & Do:

- ☐ ....
- ☐ ....
- ☐ ....
- ☐ ....
- ☐ ....
- ☐ ....
- ☐ ....
- ☐ ....
- ☐ ....
- ☐ ....

i ♡ New York

Things to Observe :

....
....
....
....
....
....
....

Adventures to Have :

....
....
....
....
....
....
....

i ♥ Travel

Places to Mingle :

....
....
....
....
....
....
....

Travel Journal

Shops to Visit :

....
....
....
....
....
....
....

Streets to Check out :

....
....
....
....
....
....
....

People to Meet :

....
....
....
....
....
....
....

Travel Journal

New York

_____
_____
_____
_____
_____
_____
_____
_____
_____
_____
_____
_____
_____
_____
_____
_____
_____
_____
_____
_____
_____

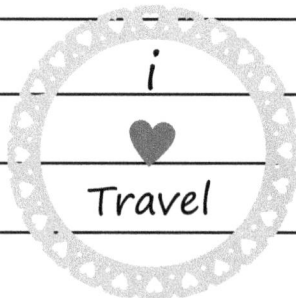

i ♥ Travel

Travel Journal

DATE: / /

Things to See & Do:

- [ ] ....
- [ ] ....
- [ ] ....
- [ ] ....
- [ ] ....
- [ ] ....
- [ ] ....
- [ ] ....
- [ ] ....
- [ ] ....

i ♥ New York

Things to Observe :

....
....
....
....
....
....
....

Adventures to Have :

....
....
....
....
....
....

i ♥ Travel

Places to Mingle :

....
....
....
....
....
....

Travel Journal

New York

Shops to Visit :

....
....
....
....
....
....
....

Streets to Check out :

....
....
....
....
....
....
....

People to Meet :

....
....
....
....
....
....
....

Travel Journal

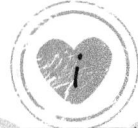 

New York

i ♥ Travel

Travel Journal

DATE: / /

New York

Things to See & Do:

- ☐ ....
- ☐ ....
- ☐ ....
- ☐ ....
- ☐ ....
- ☐ ....
- ☐ ....
- ☐ ....
- ☐ ....
- ☐ ....

Things to Observe :

....
....
....
....
....
....
....

Adventures to Have :

....
....
....
....
....
....
....

i ♥ Travel

Places to Mingle :

....
....
....
....
....
....
....

Travel Journal

New York

Shops to Visit :

....
....
....
....
....
....
....

Streets to Check out :

....
....
....
....
....
....
....

People to Meet :

....
....
....
....
....
....
....

Travel Journal

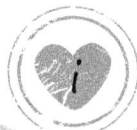

 New York

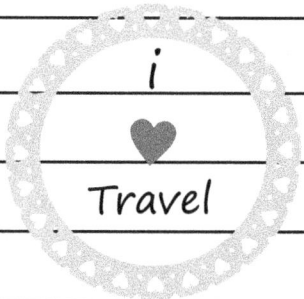

i ♥ Travel

Travel Journal

DATE: / /

i ♥ New York

Things to See & Do:

- ☐ ....
- ☐ ....
- ☐ ....
- ☐ ....
- ☐ ....
- ☐ ....
- ☐ ....
- ☐ ....
- ☐ ....
- ☐ ....

Things to Observe :

....
....
....
....
....
....
....

Adventures to Have :

....
....
....
....
....
....
....

i ♥ Travel

Places to Mingle :

....
....
....
....
....
....
....

Travel Journal

Shops to Visit :

....

....

....

....

....

....

Streets to Check out :

....

....

....

....

....

....

....

People to Meet :

....

....

....

....

....

....

Travel Journal

New York

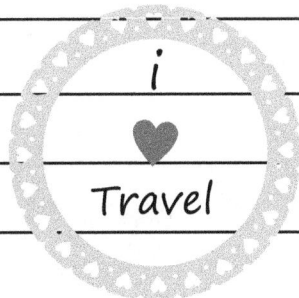

i

♥

Travel

Travel Journal

Things to See & Do:

i ♥ New York

- ☐ ....
- ☐ ....
- ☐ ....
- ☐ ....
- ☐ ....
- ☐ ....
- ☐ ....
- ☐ ....
- ☐ ....
- ☐ ....

Things to Observe :

....
....
....
....
....
....

Adventures to Have :

....
....
....
....
....
....
....

i ♥ Travel

Places to Mingle :

....
....
....
....
....
....

Travel Journal

New York

Shops to Visit :

....
....
....
....
....
....
....

Streets to Check out :

....
....
....
....
....
....
....

People to Meet :

....
....
....
....
....
....
....

Travel Journal

New York

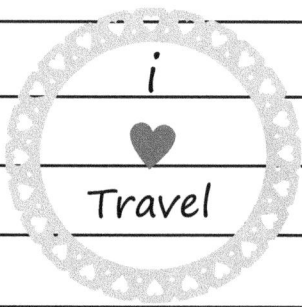

i ♥ Travel

Travel Journal

I ♥ New York

Things to See & Do:

- ☐ ....
- ☐ ....
- ☐ ....
- ☐ ....
- ☐ ....
- ☐ ....
- ☐ ....
- ☐ ....
- ☐ ....
- ☐ ....

Things to Observe :

....
....
....
....
....
....
....

Adventures to Have :

....
....
....
....
....
....
....

i ♥ Travel

Places to Mingle :

....
....
....
....
....
....
....

Travel Journal

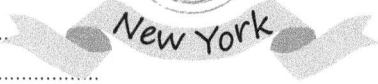

Shops to Visit :

....
....
....
....
....
....

Streets to Check out :

....
....
....
....
....
....
....

People to Meet :

....
....
....
....
....
....

Travel Journal

New York

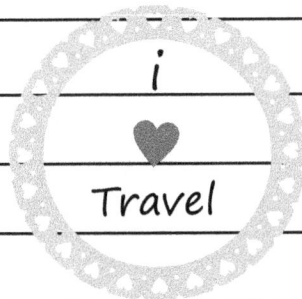

i ♥ Travel

Travel Journal

New York

Things to See & Do:

☐ ....
☐ ....
☐ ....
☐ ....
☐ ....
☐ ....
☐ ....
☐ ....
☐ ....
☐ ....

Things to Observe :

....
....
....
....
....
....
....

Adventures to Have :

....
....
....
....
....
....
....

i ♥ Travel

Places to Mingle :

....
....
....
....
....
....
....

Travel Journal

Shops to Visit :

....
....
....
....
....
....
....

Streets to Check out :

....
....
....
....
....
....
....

People to Meet :

....
....
....
....
....
....
....

Travel Journal

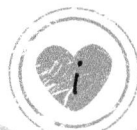

 New York

i

❤

Travel

Travel Journal

Things to See & Do.

- ☐ ....
- ☐ ....
- ☐ ....
- ☐ ....
- ☐ ....
- ☐ ....
- ☐ ....
- ☐ ....
- ☐ ....
- ☐ ....

i ♥ New York

Things to Observe :

....
....
....
....
....
....
....

Adventures to Have :

....
....
....
....
....
....
....

i ♥ Travel

Places to Mingle :

....
....
....
....
....
....
....

Travel Journal

Shops to Visit :

....
....
....
....
....
....
....

Streets to Check out :

....
....
....
....
....
....
....

People to Meet :

....
....
....
....
....
....
....

Travel Journal

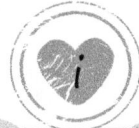

New York

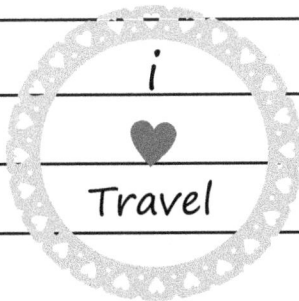

i

♥

Travel

Travel Journal

DATE: / /

Things to See & Do:

- [ ] ....
- [ ] ....
- [ ] ....
- [ ] ....
- [ ] ....
- [ ] ....
- [ ] ....
- [ ] ....
- [ ] ....
- [ ] ....

i ♥ New York

Things to Observe :

....
....
....
....
....
....
....

Adventures to Have :

....
....
....
....
....
....
....

i ♥ Travel

Places to Mingle :

....
....
....
....
....
....
....

Travel Journal

New York

Shops to Visit :

....
....
....
....
....
....
....

Streets to Check out :

....
....
....
....
....
....
....

People to Meet :

....
....
....
....
....
....
....

Travel Journal

New York

i
♥
Travel

Travel Journal

i
New York

Things to See & Do:

- ☐ ....
- ☐ ....
- ☐ ....
- ☐ ....
- ☐ ....
- ☐ ....
- ☐ ....
- ☐ ....
- ☐ ....
- ☐ ....

Things to Observe :

....
....
....
....
....
....
....

Adventures to Have :

....
....
....
....
....
....
....

i
♥
Travel

Places to Mingle :

....
....
....
....
....
....

Travel Journal

New York

Shops to Visit :

....
....
....
....
....
....
....

Streets to Check out :

....
....
....
....
....
....
....

People to Meet :

....
....
....
....
....
....

Travel Journal

New York

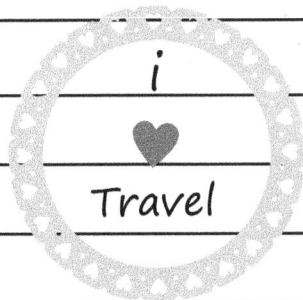

i

♥

Travel

Travel Journal

DATE: / /

Things to See & Do:

☐ ....
☐ ....
☐ ....
☐ ....
☐ ....
☐ ....
☐ ....
☐ ....
☐ ....
☐ ....

i ♥ New York

Things to Observe :

....
....
....
....
....
....
....

Adventures to Have :

....
....
....
....
....
....
....

i ♥ Travel

Places to Mingle :

....
....
....
....
....
....
....

Travel Journal

Shops to Visit :

....
....
....
....
....
....
....

Streets to Check out :

....
....
....
....
....
....
....

People to Meet :

....
....
....
....
....
....
....

Travel Journal

New York

i
♥
Travel

Travel Journal

Things to See & Do.

- ☐ ....
- ☐ ....
- ☐ ....
- ☐ ....
- ☐ ....
- ☐ ....
- ☐ ....
- ☐ ....
- ☐ ....
- ☐ ....

i ♥ New York

Things to Observe :

....
....
....
....
....
....
....
....

Adventures to Have :

....
....
....
....
....
....
....

i ♥ Travel

Places to Mingle :

....
....
....
....
....
....
....

Travel Journal

Shops to Visit :

....
....
....
....
....
....
....

Streets to Check out :

....
....
....
....
....
....
....

People to Meet :

....
....
....
....
....
....
....

Travel Journal

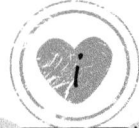 

New York

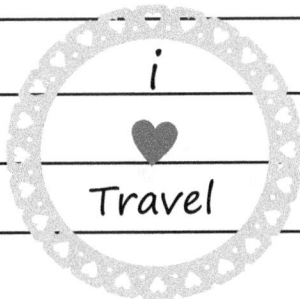

i ♥ Travel

Travel Journal

DATE: / /

Things to See & Do:

- ☐ ....
- ☐ ....
- ☐ ....
- ☐ ....
- ☐ ....
- ☐ ....
- ☐ ....
- ☐ ....
- ☐ ....
- ☐ ....

New York

Things to Observe :

....
....
....
....
....
....
....

Adventures to Have :

....
....
....
....
....
....
....

i ♥ Travel

Places to Mingle :

....
....
....
....
....
....
....

Travel Journal

Shops to Visit :

....
....
....
....
....
....
....

Streets to Check out :

....
....
....
....
....
....
....

People to Meet :

....
....
....
....
....
....
....

Travel Journal

New York

i ♥ Travel

Travel Journal

i New York

Things to See & Do:

☐ ....
☐ ....
☐ ....
☐ ....
☐ ....
☐ ....
☐ ....
☐ ....
☐ ....
☐ ....

Things to Observe :

....
....
....
....
....
....
....
....

Adventures to Have :

....
....
....
....
....
....
....

i ♥ Travel

Places to Mingle :

....
....
....
....
....
....
....

Travel Journal

Shops to Visit :

....
....
....
....
....
....
....

Streets to Check out :

....
....
....
....
....
....
....

People to Meet :

....
....
....
....
....
....
....

Travel Journal

New York

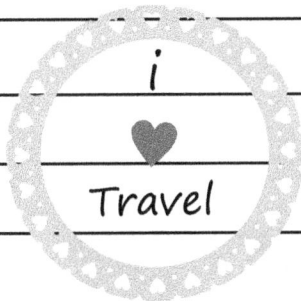

Travel Journal

New York

Things to See & Do:

☐ ....
☐ ....
☐ ....
☐ ....
☐ ....
☐ ....
☐ ....
☐ ....
☐ ....
☐ ....

Things to Observe :

....
....
....
....
....
....
....
....

Adventures to Have :

....
....
....
....
....
....
....

i ♥ Travel

Places to Mingle :

....
....
....
....
....
....
....

Travel Journal

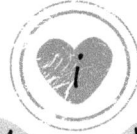 

New York

Shops to Visit :

....
....
....
....
....
....
....

Streets to Check out :

....
....
....
....
....
....
....

People to Meet :

....
....
....
....
....
....
....

Travel Journal

New York

i
♥
Travel

Travel Journal

DATE: /   /

Things to See & Do:

- [ ] ....
- [ ] ....
- [ ] ....
- [ ] ....
- [ ] ....
- [ ] ....
- [ ] ....
- [ ] ....
- [ ] ....
- [ ] ....

i ♥ New York

Things to Observe :

....
....
....
....
....
....

Adventures to Have :

....
....
....
....
....
....
....

i ♥ Travel

Places to Mingle :

....
....
....
....
....
....
....

Travel Journal

New York

Shops to Visit :

....

....

....

....

....

....

....

Streets to Check out :

....

....

....

....

....

....

....

People to Meet :

....

....

....

....

....

....

....

Travel Journal

New York

_____

_____

_____

_____

_____

_____

_____

_____

_____

_____

_____

_____

_____

_____

_____

_____

_____

_____

_____

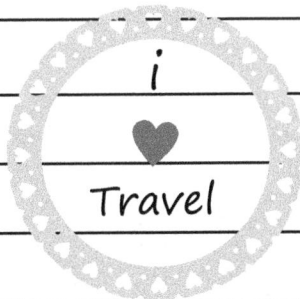
i ♥ Travel

Travel Journal

Things to See & Do:

- ☐ ....
- ☐ ....
- ☐ ....
- ☐ ....
- ☐ ....
- ☐ ....
- ☐ ....
- ☐ ....
- ☐ ....
- ☐ ....

i ♡ New York

Things to Observe :

....
....
....
....
....
....
....

Adventures to Have :

....
....
....
....
....
....
....

i ♥ Travel

Places to Mingle :

....
....
....
....
....
....
....

Travel Journal

Shops to Visit :

....
....
....
....
....
....
....

Streets to Check out :

....
....
....
....
....
....
....

People to Meet :

....
....
....
....
....
....
....

Travel Journal

New York

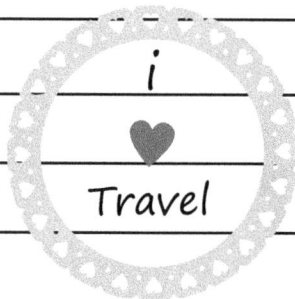

i

Travel

Travel Journal

i ♥ New York

Things to See & Do:

- ☐ ....
- ☐ ....
- ☐ ....
- ☐ ....
- ☐ ....
- ☐ ....
- ☐ ....
- ☐ ....
- ☐ ....
- ☐ ....

Things to Observe :

....
....
....
....
....
....
....

Adventures to Have :

....
....
....
....
....
....
....

i ♥ Travel

Places to Mingle :

....
....
....
....
....
....

Travel Journal

Shops to Visit :

....
....
....
....
....
....
....

Streets to Check out :

....
....
....
....
....
....
....

People to Meet :

....
....
....
....
....
....
....

Travel Journal

New York

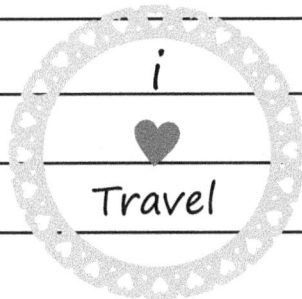

i ♥ Travel

Travel Journal

DATE: /   /

Things to See & Do:

☐ ....
☐ ....
☐ ....
☐ ....
☐ ....
☐ ....
☐ ....
☐ ....
☐ ....
☐ ....

i ♥ New York

Things to Observe :

....
....
....
....
....
....
....

Adventures to Have :

....
....
....
....
....
....
....

i ♥ Travel

Places to Mingle :

....
....
....
....
....
....
....

Travel Journal

Shops to Visit :

....
....
....
....
....
....
....

Streets to Check out :

....
....
....
....
....
....
....

People to Meet :

....
....
....
....
....
....

Travel Journal

New York

i ♥ Travel

Travel Journal

DATE: /   /

Things to See & Do:

- ☐ ....
- ☐ ....
- ☐ ....
- ☐ ....
- ☐ ....
- ☐ ....
- ☐ ....
- ☐ ....
- ☐ ....
- ☐ ....

New York

Things to Observe :

....
....
....
....
....
....

Adventures to Have :

....
....
....
....
....
....
....

i ♥ Travel

Places to Mingle :

....
....
....
....
....
....
....

Travel Journal

Shops to Visit :

....
....
....
....
....
....

Streets to Check out :

....
....
....
....
....
....
....

People to Meet :

....
....
....
....
....
....

Travel Journal

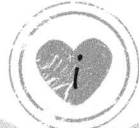

New York

_____

_____

_____

_____

_____

_____

_____

_____

_____

_____

_____

_____

_____

_____

_____

_____

_____

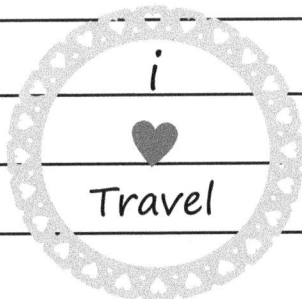

i ♥ Travel

Travel Journal

DATE: / /

Things to See & Do:

- ☐ ....
- ☐ ....
- ☐ ....
- ☐ ....
- ☐ ....
- ☐ ....
- ☐ ....
- ☐ ....
- ☐ ....
- ☐ ....

New York

Things to Observe :

....
....
....
....
....
....
....

Adventures to Have :

....
....
....
....
....
....
....

i ♥ Travel

Places to Mingle :

....
....
....
....
....
....
....

Travel Journal

Shops to Visit :

....
....
....
....
....
....

Streets to Check out :

....
....
....
....
....
....

People to Meet :

....
....
....
....
....
....

Travel Journal

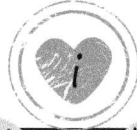

New York

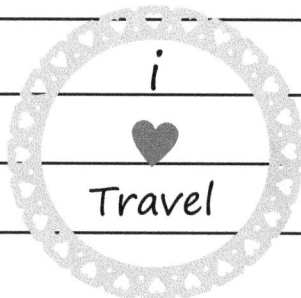
i ♥ Travel

Travel Journal

i ♥ New York

Things to See & Do.

☐ ....
☐ ....
☐ ....
☐ ....
☐ ....
☐ ....
☐ ....
☐ ....
☐ ....
☐ ....

Things to Observe :

....
....
....
....
....
....
....

Adventures to Have :

....
....
....
....
....
....
....

i ♥ Travel

Places to Mingle :

....
....
....
....
....
....
....

Travel Journal

Shops to Visit :

....
....
....
....
....
....
....

Streets to Check out :

....
....
....
....
....
....
....

People to Meet :

....
....
....
....
....
....
....

Travel Journal

New York

i
❤
Travel

Travel Journal

Things to See & Do:

- [ ] ....
- [ ] ....
- [ ] ....
- [ ] ....
- [ ] ....
- [ ] ....
- [ ] ....
- [ ] ....
- [ ] ....
- [ ] ....

New York

Things to Observe :

....
....
....
....
....
....

Adventures to Have :

....
....
....
....
....
....
....

i ♥ Travel

Places to Mingle :

....
....
....
....
....
....
....

Travel Journal

New York

Shops to Visit :

....
....
....
....
....
....

Streets to Check out :

....
....
....
....
....
....

People to Meet :

....
....
....
....
....
....

Travel Journal

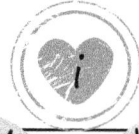

New York

i
♥
Travel

Travel Journal

New York

Things to See & Do.

- ☐ ....
- ☐ ....
- ☐ ....
- ☐ ....
- ☐ ....
- ☐ ....
- ☐ ....
- ☐ ....
- ☐ ....
- ☐ ....

Things to Observe :

....
....
....
....
....
....

Adventures to Have :

....
....
....
....
....
....
....

i ♥ Travel

Places to Mingle :

....
....
....
....
....
....
....

Travel Journal

Shops to Visit :

....
....
....
....
....
....

Streets to Check out :

....
....
....
....
....
....
....

People to Meet :

....
....
....
....
....
....

Travel Journal

New York

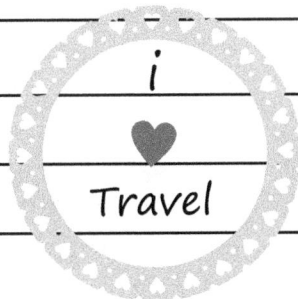

i ♥ Travel

Travel Journal

DATE: / /

Things to See & Do:

☐ ....
☐ ....
☐ ....
☐ ....
☐ ....
☐ ....
☐ ....
☐ ....
☐ ....
☐ ....

i ♥ New York

Things to Observe :

....
....
....
....
....
....
....

Adventures to Have :

....
....
....
....
....
....
....

i ♥ Travel

Places to Mingle :

....
....
....
....
....
....
....

Travel Journal

Shops to Visit :

....
....
....
....
....
....

Streets to Check out :

....
....
....
....
....
....
....

People to Meet :

....
....
....
....
....
....
....

Travel Journal

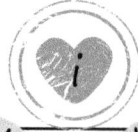

New York

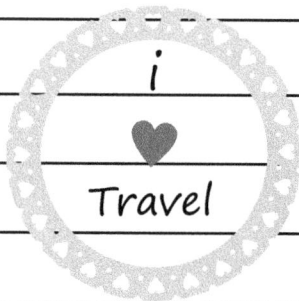
i ♥ Travel

Travel Journal

i ♥ New York

Things to See & Do.

☐ ....
☐ ....
☐ ....
☐ ....
☐ ....
☐ ....
☐ ....
☐ ....
☐ ....
☐ ....

Things to Observe :

....
....
....
....
....
....
....
....

Adventures to Have :

....
....
....
....
....
....
....

i ♥ Travel

Places to Mingle :

....
....
....
....
....
....
....

Travel Journal

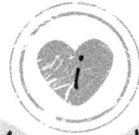

Shops to Visit :

....
....
....
....
....
....

Streets to Check out :

....
....
....
....
....
....

People to Meet :

....
....
....
....
....
....

Travel Journal

New York

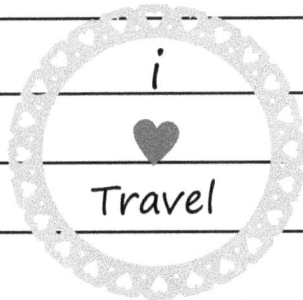

i

♥

Travel

Travel Journal

Things to See & Do:

- ☐ ....
- ☐ ....
- ☐ ....
- ☐ ....
- ☐ ....
- ☐ ....
- ☐ ....
- ☐ ....
- ☐ ....
- ☐ ....

i ❤ New York

Things to Observe :

....
....
....
....
....
....
....

Adventures to Have :

....
....
....
....
....
....
....

i ❤ Travel

Places to Mingle :

....
....
....
....
....
....
....

Travel Journal

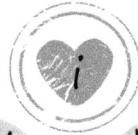 

New York

Shops to Visit :

....
....
....
....
....
....
....

Streets to Check out :

....
....
....
....
....
....
....

People to Meet :

....
....
....
....
....
....
....

Travel Journal

New York

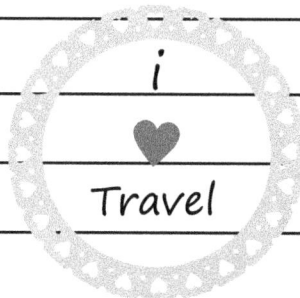

i ♥ Travel

Travel Journal

Things to See & Do:

- ☐ ....
- ☐ ....
- ☐ ....
- ☐ ....
- ☐ ....
- ☐ ....
- ☐ ....
- ☐ ....
- ☐ ....
- ☐ ....

i ♡ New York

Things to Observe :

....
....
....
....
....
....
....

Adventures to Have :

....
....
....
....
....
....
....

i ♥ Travel

Places to Mingle :

....
....
....
....
....
....
....

Travel Journal

Shops to Visit :

....
....
....
....
....
....

Streets to Check out :

....
....
....
....
....
....

People to Meet :

....
....
....
....
....
....

Travel Journal

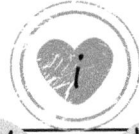
New York

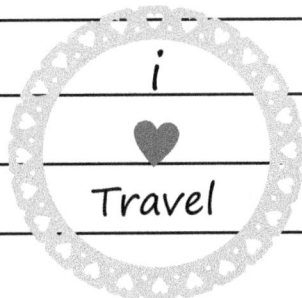
i ♥ Travel

www.ingramcontent.com/pod-product-compliance
Lightning Source LLC
Chambersburg PA
CBHW081334090426
42737CB00017B/3140